101 Facts About

RABBITS

Published by Ringpress Books Limited,
PO Box 8, Lydney, Gloucestershire,
GL15 4YN, United Kingdom.

Design: Sara Howell

First Published 2001
© 2001 RINGPRESS BOOKS LIMITED

ISBN 1 86054 133 X

Printed in Hong Kong through Printworks Int. Ltd.

0 9 8 7 6 5 4 3 2 1

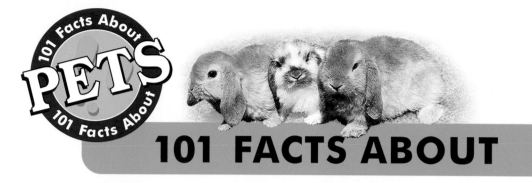

101 Facts About **PETS** · 101 Facts About

101 FACTS ABOUT

RABBITS

Julia Barnes

Ringpress Books

1 Rabbits have been around for a very long time – the remains of rabbits have been found in Spain and Portugal from 4,000 years ago.

2 About 2,000 years ago, the Romans reared rabbits for meat and fur and kept them in walled enclosures called *leporia*.

3 People started keeping rabbits as pets just over 200 years ago. They are now one of the most popular of all the small animals to keep.

4 Rabbits belong to the *Lagomorpha* family. They are more closely related to hoofed animals (such as horses) than to the rodent family, which includes many of the other small animals kept as pets (such as rats, mice, hamsters and guinea pigs).

5 Although hares are reckoned to be their closest relative, rabbits cannot run as fast. The hare can reach speeds of 50 miles an hour (80 km per hour), whereas the rabbit has to rely on twisting and turning to escape his enemies before finding safety underground.

6 The name 'rabbit' comes from 'robbe', an old Dutch word for anyone called Robert. Bunny comes from the word 'bun' which means 'squirrel' in some parts of England.

7 In the wild, rabbits live in groups with around 8 to 15 members.

10 Wild rabbits sleep during the day and come out to feed at dawn and at dusk.

11 Three rabbits will eat as much grass in a day as one sheep, making them a serious pest to farmers.

8 There is usually a top-ranking male (**buck**) and a top-ranking female (**doe**) in each group.

9 Rabbits live in complex underground **warrens**, which have several exit tunnels.

6

12 Rabbits make excellent pets for children as they are easy to handle and care for, and they can live in outdoor housing.

13 The average pet rabbit will live for six to eight years.

14 The oldest rabbit on record is Flopsy, a wild rabbit caught in Tasmania, Australia, and kept as a pet until it died aged 18 years and 11 months.

15 All pet rabbits are descended from the European wild rabbit.

16 Special breeding programmes have produced lots of different rabbit breeds. There are now some 50 breeds, and about 80 varieties to choose from.

17 Rabbits range in size from the **giant breeds**, such as the Flemish Giant, weighing around 25 lbs (11.3 kgs), to the popular **dwarf breeds**, such as the Netherland Dwarf (below), which weighs around 2 lbs (0.9 kgs).

18 Nearly all pet rabbits (including the dwarf breeds) are bigger than their wild ancestors.

19 Pet rabbits are divided into four main types: **Normal Fur, Rex, Satin,** and **Fancy Breed**.

20 The **Satin** type has a flat, shiny coat in a wide range of colours, and includes the Argent, Himalayan and the Opal.

21 **Rex** rabbits have a shorter, velvety coat; breeds include the Self, the Shaded and the Tan.

23 The **Normal Fur** group has a coat that is about one inch (2.5 cms) long – the same as a wild rabbit. The Chinchilla, the Havana, and the New Zealand are among the many breeds in this group.

22 The **Fancy Breeds** cover a wide range which includes the Netherland Dwarf, the English lop, and the longcoated Angora (above).

▲ Chinchilla

Havana ▶

24 Some rabbit breeds have drooping ears and they are known as lops. They include the Dwarf lop (above), which makes an ideal pet.

25 The English lop's ears (measured from the tip of one ear to the tip of the other) can be as much as 28 ins (70 cms) long. The ears can be very delicate, and spacious accommodation is needed so the rabbit does not tread on his ears.

26 There are lots of different colours to choose from. Pet rabbits can be agouti, which is the brown-grey colour of the wild rabbit.

27 Other colours include black, white, blue, lilac, chocolate, sooty and fawn, and chinchilla (which appears silver-coloured).

to breed, and some are not so suitable to keep as pets.

30 The best pet breeds include the lively Dutch, which weighs around 5lbs (2.7 kgs), the Himalayan, which is bigger but has a calm, gentle nature, and the Netherland Dwarf.

28 Markings can be spectacular. They include Sealpoint/Sablepoint (markings like a Siamese cat), Dalmatian (white body with spots/ blotches), Magpie (a colour and white), and Harlequin (a colour and orange or fawn, above).

29 The character (temperament) of a rabbit can vary from breed

31 Avoid the Angora, unless you want to spend all your time grooming, and the Britannia Petite/Polish which can have a nasty temper.

32 **Crossbred** rabbits also make good pets, but, if you are choosing a young rabbit, you will not know what size it will be, or what its character will be like.

33 The best age to buy a rabbit is around eight weeks of age so it will get used to being handled.

34 The best place to go for your rabbit is a well-run pet store where experienced staff can help you. If you want to get involved in showing rabbits, you will need to find a breeder that specialises in producing **pedigree/pure-bred** rabbits.

35 The signs of a healthy rabbit are:

- Body: Well covered and rounded. No abnormal swellings.
- Breathing: Quiet/regular.
- Ears: Ear flaps undamaged. No discharge or redness in the ear canals.
- Eyes: Bright and clear, without any discharge.
- Nose: Clean and free from discharge.
- Mouth: The teeth should not be overgrown. Dribbling can be a sign of problems.
- Coat: Well-groomed. Should not be dirty or matted.

36 Rabbits do not always get on well with each other. Two bucks are likely to fight.

37 A **doe** and a **buck** will get on fine – but they will produce lots of baby rabbits...

38 An experienced rabbit-keeper will show you how to tell which rabbit is male, and which is female.

39 Rabbits can be kept in an outdoor **hutch**, or you may prefer to keep your rabbit indoors and train it to be a **house-rabbit**.

40 An outdoor hutch should be as big as possible. It should be raised at least 9 ins (23 cms) off the ground to prevent dampness and draughts.

41 The hutch should have a separate sleeping compartment, and a secure wire front to prevent rats and mice from getting in.

42 On cold nights, heavy sacking placed on top of the hutch will provide extra warmth.

44 If you are keeping your rabbit in the house, it will need a large wire cage, with a resting board covering the wire floor. The most convenient bedding to use is shredded paper.

45 Both hutch and cage must have a supply of fresh water. This is best provided by a water-bottle.

43 Rabbits appreciate a nice, deep bed. This can be made from wood shavings or straw, with some additional hay which can be eaten and used for bedding.

46 In the warm weather, rabbits love to be outside in an exercise run.

47 The run should be as big as possible, and it must have access to shade. A water-bottle must be attached to the side of the run.

48 Place some lengths of pipe in the run and construct a maze for your rabbit to enjoy tunnelling in and out.

49 It is important to rabbit-proof your home if you are allowing your rabbit to run free in selected areas. Electrical cables are the chief problem, but house plants can also be dangerous.

50 Remember that rabbits love to gnaw – so make sure your rabbit cannot do any damage to furniture.

playing with empty cardboard boxes if you cut doors and windows for them to hop in and out of.

51 House-rabbits should have their own cushions which they are allowed to use, or you can cover your own furniture with old material or towels to prevent damage.

52 House-rabbits also need toys to play with. The most popular is a football, which they can push and roll. They will also enjoy

53 In the wild, rabbits have 'toilet areas', and so it is not difficult to train a rabbit to use a litter tray. Be patient, and never tell off your rabbit for making a mistake.

17

54 Rabbits have a very good sense of taste. They have 17,000 taste buds in their mouth compared to 10,000 in humans.

55 A wild rabbit's diet includes a wide variety of plants and vegetables, but it is best to feed a pet rabbit on a complete or pelleted diet that is specially designed to meet their needs.

56 Your rabbit will also appreciate some fresh food, such as carrots, cauliflower, cabbage, sprouts, swede and turnip.

57 Hay is an essential part of a pet rabbit's diet. Make sure it is fresh and sweet-smelling before giving it to your rabbit.

60 Give your rabbit a chance to settle when he first arrives home. Watch how he behaves, and you will learn to understand him.

61 A rabbit can move his ears in all directions, and he is very sensitive to sound. Try to avoid making sudden noises that will frighten your rabbit.

58 Avoid feeding lettuce – it has little food value, and too much will cause diarrhoea.

59 Do not leave food lying around in the hutch or cage. Rotting food can cause serious illness.

19

62 Rabbits can see to the front, to the sides, and to the rear — essential for spotting an enemy approaching. But they have poor close-up sight, and you will be surprised at how they may fail to spot nearby objects.

63 A rabbit's sense of touch comes from his whiskers, which are as long as his body is wide. They are used to measure the width of tunnels in the warren, and for finding the way in the dark.

64 If you see a rabbit rubbing his chin against objects, it means he is marking his territory with his own scent — but you will not be able to smell it.

65 In the morning, you may see a rabbit eating his droppings. This is not a bad habit – the lighter-coloured droppings passed at night are needed to help the rabbit digest his food.

66 In the wild, rabbits warn each other of approaching danger by thumping their back feet. A pet rabbit may do this if he is frightened, or a bossy rabbit may use it as a threat.

67 Lying flat on the ground is a way of trying to be invisible to enemies. If you see a rabbit doing this, he is probably very frightened.

68 If a rabbit rises up on his haunches, he is trying to get a better view, sniff out a scent, or reach a tempting treat.

69 Verbal language also communicates feelings. A rabbit that is muttering, making a short, scolding noise, is either angry or is issuing a warning.

70 Hissing (which sounds like a hissing cat) is a sign of aggression, and the rabbit may be about to attack.

71 A soft grinding of teeth means your rabbit is content. He may do this when you stroke him.

72 Loud squealing means your rabbit is in terrible pain or in great danger.

73 The more you handle your rabbit, the tamer he will become. Hand-feeding is a good way of making friends.

74 Remember, rabbits are nervous animals, and must be handled firmly but gently.

attempt this, make sure you are sitting on the floor to avoid accidents.

76 The other safe method is to hold the rabbit facing away from you. Have one hand under his front legs, and the other hand supporting his rear.

75 Never lift a rabbit up by his ears. The correct way to pick up a rabbit is to get hold of the scruff of the neck with one hand, and then place your other hand to support his hindquarters. When you first

77 Using lots of food treats and lots of patience, rabbits will learn to respond to a number of verbal commands.

23

78 You can teach your rabbit to "Come" (come to you), "Go home" (return to his hutch or cage), and to "Be clean" (use his litter tray).

79 "No" is an essential command for the house-rabbit to stop any bad behaviour. Use a firm tone of voice, and repeat the command every time your rabbit misbehaves. It won't be long before he understands what you mean.

80 Rabbits are easy to look after if they are given the correct diet and an environment that suits them.

81 The hutch or cage needs to be kept clean at all times. Every day, droppings and wet bedding need to be removed, the feeding bowls need to be cleaned, and fresh water should be given.

85 If the front teeth do grow too long, it will be very uncomfortable for your rabbit. The signs are: difficulty in eating and drooling saliva. Your vet will be able to cut the teeth back.

82 Every week, remove all the bedding and give a thorough clean-out.

83 A rabbit's front (incisor) teeth can grow by as much as five inches (12.7 cms) in one year.

84 Constant gnawing on hard food, such as carrots, will keep a rabbit's teeth in trim.

86 Nails are kept in trim by scratching and digging. If they grow too long, your vet or an experienced rabbit-keeper will be able to trim them using nail-clippers.

87 The amount of grooming a rabbit needs depends on the length of coat. A shorthaired rabbit (below) only needs to be brushed when the coat is shedding – usually once or twice a year.

88 A longhaired rabbit, such as a Cashmere Lop (above), needs brushing at least once a week.

89 The exotic Angora needs constant grooming, as well as special housing to prevent the coat from getting dirty and matted.

90 If a rabbit is unwell, he may show some of the following signs:
- Runny eyes or nose
- Drooling or difficulty eating
- Heavy breathing
- A matted, dirty coat
- Loss of appetite
- Drinking more than normal
- Diarrhoea
- Discharge from the ears.
  If you spot any of these signs, consult a vet.

91 If a rabbit is eating normally, but does not look healthy, he may have worms. Ask your vet to prescribe a suitable worming treatment.

92 Pet rabbits should be vaccinated against myxomatosis and viral haemorrhagic disease – infectious diseases that are usually fatal. Ask your vet for advice.

95 Pregnancy (gestation) lasts around one month, and the young are usually born at night.

93 Does can breed at all times of the year; in the wild, they may have many litters a year, each with around five babies.

96 Baby rabbits are born without fur, they are blind, and they cannot hear.

94 The record for producing the most young goes to superdad Chewer, a Norfolk Star buck who fathered 40,000 offspring between 1968 and 1973.

100 At two months of age, the rabbits will be fully independent, and are ready to go to new homes.

97 Within seven days, the fur starts to grow, and they have doubled in weight.

101 Rabbits are delightful pets to keep – and the more time you spend with your rabbit, the more rewarding your relationship will be.

98 The eyes open at around 10 days, and the baby rabbits can hear at 12 days.

99 By 18 days, they will be eating solid food.

GLOSSARY

Buck: a male rabbit.

Crossbred: a rabbit whose parents are different breeds.

Doe: a female rabbit.

Dwarf breeds: types of small rabbits.

Fancy breeds: a group of rabbits which includes the Netherland Dwarf and English lop.

Giant breeds: types of very large rabbits.

House-rabbit: a rabbit that lives indoors with its human family.

Hutch: an outdoor rabbit house.

Lagomorpha family: a group of hoofed animals that includes the horse and the rabbit.

Leporia: walled enclosures in which the Romans kept rabbits.

Lop: a rabbit with droopy ears.

Normal fur: a rabbit that has one-inch (2.5-cm) fur.

Pedigree/pure-bred: a rabbit whose parents are both the same breed.

Rex: a rabbit with a short, velvety coat.

Satin: a rabbit that has a flat, shiny coat.

Warren: a rabbit's underground house. It has several openings and lots of tunnels.

MORE BOOKS TO READ

*Pet Owner's Guide
to the Rabbit*
Marianne Mays
(Ringpress Books)

*Pet Owner's Guide
to the Dwarf Rabbit*
Hazel Lee Wood
(Ringpress Books)

All About Your Rabbit
Bradley Viner
(Ringpress Books)

Rabbits (Perfect Pet Series)
Kathryn Hinds
(Marshall Cavendish)

WEBSITES

Rabbits
www.ukpet.rabbits.org.uk/

British house-rabbit
www.houserabbit.co.uk

American house-rabbit
www.houserabbit.org/kids

Rabbits online
www.rabbitsonline.com

To find additional websites, use a reliable search engine to find one or more of the following key words: **rabbits, rabbit care, bunnies.**

INDEX